PRAISE

"What a joy it is reading this marvelous book about boozing! It's craftily written with lots of fine drink recipes, and the drawings are charming in an innocent, homemade way. Good book!"

—Tony Millionaire, cartoonist, author of *Maakies*

"Luckily for me I drink. Professionally. Take my advice and have a well-made tipple on hand while thumbing through this book. At least you'll have that going for you. In a pinch, tear out the pages, as they seem to be absorbent and make adequate cocktail napkins."

—Charles Joly, award-winning mixologist, co-founder of Crafthouse Cocktails

"*Cocktails for Ding Dongs* is the bar book equivalent of a flamingo swizzle stick: if truly delicious cocktails weren't enough to get you in a good mood, Drankiewicz's hilarious recipes and Ensign's playful comics will surely do the trick. Now go get some booze, your strainer, and your shaker and have some fun, you dumb dumb!"

—Marnie Galloway, cartoonist, author of *In the Sounds and Seas*

"Dustin Drankiewicz brings a laid-back approach to cocktail making that sways from the pretentiousness that many in the libation field would be quick to learn from. Simple, well-thought-out flavor combinations and a nod to the classics will make *Cocktails for Ding Dongs* a classic book to draw influence for your next dinner party or drunkening event!"

—Jared Wentworth, Michelin-starred chef (Dusek's, Longman & Eagle)

"This book is like the endearing nutty character that hangs out at your favorite old bar. If you don't find this book funny, have another drink because you need it. I love the quirky cartoons that accompany each drink recipe. It's a delightful treat for any drink aficionado."

—Robin Ha, author and illustrator of *Cook Korean!: A Comic Book With Recipes*

COCKTAILS

FOR DING DONGS

RECIPES BY DUSTIN DRANKIEWICZ

COMICS BY ALEXANDRA ENSIGN

CURBSIDE SPLENDOR PUBLISHING

Published by Curbside Splendor Publishing, Inc., Chicago, Illinois in 2016.

First Edition
Copyright © 2016 by Dustin Drankiewicz and Alexandra Ensign
Library of Congress Control Number: 2016946771

ISBN 978-1940430850
Design by Alexandra Ensign

Manufactured in the United States of America.

www.curbsidesplendor.com
www.16oncenterchicago.com

TABLE OF CONTENTS

FOREWORD
BY JAKE AUSTEN

Despite being alliteratively compatible, crafty cocktails rarely grab the empty barstool next to kooky comics. It's not that cartoonists are strangers to alcoholism (I'd put Wally Wood's cirrhosis against Charles Bukowski's any day). It's just that the social aspect of going out for exquisitely constructed libations in friendly taverns is alien to most ink jockeys. This is because practitioners of this solitary, laborious, under-appreciated art form don't have a lot of free time, don't have a lot of money, and (in a tears-of-a-clown twist), usually don't have a lot of friends.

Unless they take up a hobby. Which is where our story (let's call it, "When Alex Met Dustin") begins. Although I'd seen Alex Ensign selling her mini-comics at zine festivals for a few years, I didn't become a real fan until she started barbacking at our neighborhood watering hole. With a palette as exquisite as her linework, Ensign quickly moved up to bartending, and all of a sudden, in addition to the utterly delicious cocktail wizardry of legendary lead bartender, Dustin "Don't Call Me Mixologist" Drankiewicz, I was also enjoying Ensign's concoctions. The rookie deftly applied the same craftsmanship and whimsy to her cocktails as to her cartoons. Under the tutelage of a veteran bartender with a reverent sense of booze history, an irreverent sense of humor, and a deep appreciation of the everyman's dive bar experience, Ensign improved her chops, and found in Dusto an enthusiastic audience for her libation-themed illustrations.

Their inevitable collaboration, *Cocktails for Ding Dongs*, puts the "fun" in "functional." If it were just a pamphlet in which one of the Midwest's most brilliant beverage builders shared trade secrets, this would be as valuable as Houdini whispering into your ear which orifices work best for hiding lock picks. But alongside these tremendous recipes (presented in a conversational, goofy voice, generous with knowledge accrued over years of liver damage) are illustrated gag cartoons that visually surpass even the pink elephants of boozehound cartoon lore. Ensign's wacky anthropomorphic menagerie brings the spirit of Dustin's spirits to life with a sense of political, cultural, and satirical modernity. The artwork also captures the elegance of the illustrators whose comics graced the age of jazz age issues of the *New Yorker*, which compliments the classic cocktails at the heart of Drankiewicz's dranks. Your senses of sight, taste and humor are all treated to a solid century of sauciness.

So make these drinks at home and impress your friends, your partners, and your taste buds. Look at these drawings and excite whatever brain lobe is connected to your funnybone. Or just bring this handsome volume to your corner gin joint and show it off; you can share some knowledge, make some new friends, and if you're lucky, maybe get laid.

Even if you're a cartoonist.

Jake Austen is an independent music writer and the editor of *Roctober* magazine. He is the author of *TV-a-Go-Go: Rock on TV from American Bandstand to American Idol*, the editor of *A Friendly Game of Poker: 52 Takes on the Neighborhood Game*, and a founder and co-host of the cult-favorite dance show *Chic-a-Go-Go*, which airs on Chicago Access Network Television (CAN-TV).

INTRODUCTION

If this book has found its way into your hands a few things may be going on:

1) Aunt Miriam was on the prowl to get you a "hip" present and saw the word "cocktails" on a book that seemed sassy. Feel free to re-gift this; we don't give a shit.

2) You are an inspiring "mixologist" and someone referred you to this elevated piece of literature to throw in your rolodex of cocktail knowledge. This isn't really that type of book.

3) You are a smart ass who enjoys the hooch and manipulating it into no-nonsense, easy-to-make, delicious cocktails to force feed to your loved ones while being insulted ever-so-sassily by a couple of ding dongs.

Whichever it is, let's keep a few things in mind. First of all, we mean no harm. We have compiled a bunch of classic cocktails, added our own twist, and inked some comics we find hilarious. We hope these recipes will help you to get over a broken heart or (better yet) break one, impress your family and friends who think you "haven't found your calling" or rely on you to handle the booze at get togethers, or help make sense of the unbelievable variety of liquor that exists on this planet. All said and done, you own this book, and because of that, you're automatically better than any other self-titled "bartender."

Here are a few tricks and tips to making it through this book, in no particular order, but numbered anyhow:

1) Upon moments of confusion, whether it be booze-, glassware- or tool-related, please reference our illustrated glossary located on page 99 in the back of this book.

2) When a recipe instructs you to *juice*, make sure you are squeezing and producing your own fresh juice. This requires a hand press (see the glossary if you don't know what the hell this is). Don't let us catch you mixing a "lemon" juice from a plastic

squeeze bottle with fine ass liquor.

3) Always double strain when we suggest it in the recipes. This will keep your cocktail smoother and colder longer! It will also make you look like you know how to walk and chew gum at the same time.

4) When stirring, look for *frost lines* in the glass. This means the cocktail has reached the proper temperature. It should take around thirty seconds.

5) When shaking, use enough ice (2/3 full is a good amount) in a Boston shaker and give yourself adequate time—roughly fifteen to twenty seconds—to allow the cocktail to reach the proper temperature. If your hands are freezing, you nailed it! When we say *dry shake,* we mean the ingredients need to be shaken without ice so the egg will emulsify (you don't need to worry about what that means for it to work—just know it makes the magic happen). Dry shake for ten to fifteen seconds, then add ice and shake again for fifteen to twenty seconds. You can get away with not dry shaking, but trust us, it's worth it.

6) *Swaths* are used to express oils over a cocktail. Use a wide peeler to remove the rind or skin of the fruit, and keep those digits out of the way. Dustin lost a nail to a nasty 'tini once. With your pointer finger and thumb of each hand, hold the swath at each end. In one motion, pinch the swath end to end and move it over the glass (see illustration). If you do

this correctly, the oils from the rind will spray onto the surface of the cocktail. Run the swath around the rim of the glass afterward to line with oils, give it one last twist, and drop it in the cocktail as directed. Instant class!

7) Don't shy away from the jigger: it's there to make sure every cocktail is balanced and consistent, no matter how shit faced you get.

Have fun, be responsible, and drink up, ding dong!

— DUSTIN & ALEX

CHAPTER ONE:
CLASS(ICS) IN SESSION

In a book full of classic cocktails, we consider this chapter to contain the essential categories or preparation of those classics, sometimes with a twist. Don't be scared, dingaling. With the right booze and tools, you got this! Just remember: these are classics, and they have withstood the test of time. Respect that, and godspeed.

HEARTH MANHATTAN

Hearth Manhattan

3 dashes Bitter Cube Vanilla-Cherry Bark Bitters
1 oz Smoked Vermouth*
2 oz Rebel Yell Rye Whiskey
cherry

Stir 'til it hurts, ding dong. Strain into a footed rocks glass.
Garnish with a cherry.

*Smoked Vermouth

1 bottle sweet vermouth
1 hearty handful hickory wood
1 smoking gun

Don't burn the house down, dumb dumb. Smoke hickory into an
airtight vessel (such as a mason jar) where you add the vermouth.
(A smoking gun tool is great for this.) Swirl the vessel for fifteen to
twenty seconds, air out the smoke, and use within thirty days. If
you can't afford a fancy ass smoking gun, add a few pieces of all
natural wood charcoal to infuse it and leave it for a few days to a
week. Taste it periodically and remove the charcoal when you've
got it where you like it (and don't forget to strain with a cheese
cloth to remove any charcoal remnants).

Tools: mixing glass, bar spoon, jigger, julep strainer, smoking gun

THE WOODED ISLE

Demetrius M. Green, 1987 – 2015

Wooded Isle

1 egg white
½ oz lemon juice
¾ oz Saigon Syrup*
¾ oz Zucca Amaro Liqueur
1½ oz Cutty Sark Blended Scotch
1 dash Angostura Bitters
1 sprig rosemary

Dry shake all that shit, except the bitters and rosemary. Add ice and shake it again. Double strain into a footed rocks glass—or a coffee mug—I don't care. Garnish with a drop of Angostura and some flamed rosemary. Seriously, light a match and run it under the rosemary. You'll know it's working when the room starts to smell like Christmas.

*Saigon Syrup

2 c demerara sugar
2 c hot water
4 cinnamon sticks

Take some sugar and water and cinnamon sticks and put the shit in a saucepan. Let it simmer so the sugar melts, then take that shit off the heat and let it cool, dingaling!

Tools: shaker tin, hawthorne strainer, fine strainer, jigger, matches

Pink Squirrel

1 oz crème de noyaux liqueur
1 oz crème de cacao liqueur
2 oz C.R.E.A.M.
cherry

Combine the first three ingredients with a big ass scoop of ice in a blender. Blend that shit until smooth and serve in a hurricane glass. Garnish with a cherry.

Tools: blender, jigger, crazy straw

EL DIABLO

El Diablo

½ oz lime juice
½ oz Combier Fruits de Rouge Liqueur
¼ oz mezcal
1½ oz Suerte Reposado Tequila
1 bottle ginger beer
lime

Shake that shit up. Pour it over some ice in a collins glass.
Top with ginger beer. Garnish with a lime wheel.

Tools: shaker tin, hawthorne strainer, jigger

THE CHILEAN SOUR

Chilean Sour

2 oz Control Pisco
1 oz lemon juice
1 oz Saigon Syrup*
1 egg white
1 muddled fig
5 drops Scrappy's Chocolate Bitters

Smash a fig to smithereens in the shaker tin. If you don't have a muddler, a wooden spoon or an empty beer bottle works, too. Dry shake. Add ice, shake, and double strain. Bitters on top. And stop whining about the egg white. It's extra protein!

Tools: shaker tin, jigger, hawthorne strainer, fine strainer, muddler

See Wooded Isle, page 15

SAZERAC

Sazerac

6 dashes Peychaud's Bitters
¼ oz House Sugar*
2 oz Hennessy VSOP Cognac
dash of absinthe
lemon

Stir 'til it hurts, ding dong. Chill a rocks glass while you're doing it. Empty the glass and rinse with a dash of absinthe. (Letherbee Absinthe is the shit.) Strain that shit and zest with two lemon swaths.

*House Sugar

1 c honey
3 c raw sugar
1 qt water
1 orange peel

Take some honey, take some raw sugar, and take the peel from an orange. Add that shit together in a saucepan, simmer it for a few minutes, and let it cool.

Tools: mixing glass, bar spoon, jigger, julep strainer, wide peeler

WHITE RUM, ED HAMILTON
BLACK CASK, HOUSE SUGAR,
LA COLOMBE COFFEE BITTERS

JAMAICAN OLD FASHIONED

Jamaican Old Fashioned

3 dashes coffee bitters
¼ oz House Sugar*
½ oz Ed Hamilton Black Cask Rum
1½ oz Brugal Extra Dry White Rum
Orange

Stir 'til it hurts, dumb dumb. Strain that shit over ice in a double
old fashioned glass. Run an orange swath around the rim, give
it a twist, and drop it in. Look up Louise "Miss Lou" Bennett-
Coverley while you sip.

Tools: mixing glass, bar spoon, jigger, julep strainer, wide peeler

*See Sazerac, page 23

Tack Room Buck

1½ oz Rebel Yell Bourbon
½ oz lemon juice
3 oz Carrot-Ginger Beer*
mint

Put the bourbon and lemon juice in a glass full of ice. Top with Carrot-Ginger Beer. Throw some mint in that shit for aromatics.

*Carrot-Ginger Beer

1 c ginger
12 carrots (juiced)
3 c sugar
2 oz citric acid
peels from 2 lemons and 2 oranges

You're probably super hip so grab your juice extractor... We'll wait. Okay, now peel and juice the carrots. Take that shit and put it into a sauce pan with peels from the oranges and lemons and one big ass cup of pulverized (or just finely chopped) ginger root. After it starts to simmer, add some sugar and citric acid. Let that mellow out, buddy, and then fine strain it. Use an ISI to carbonate it.

Tools: ISI, jigger, juicer, paring knife, wide peeler

THE SMOKE & MIRRORS

Smoke & Mirrors

¾ oz lemon juice
¾ oz Honey Mix*
3 dashes Angostura Bitters
3 dashes Laphroaig Scotch Whiskey
2 oz white port
lemon
fresh thyme

Shake that shit and double strain into a footed rocks glass.
Garnish with a sprig of fresh thyme wrapped in a lemon twist,
dumb dumb.

*Honey Mix

Mix two parts honey with one part hot water until melted. Keeps
in the fridge for weeks. Makes a dope waffle dipping sauce.

Tools: shaker tin, jigger, hawthorne strainer, fine strainer,
channel knife

GIN & TONIG

Gin & Tonic

1 ½ oz Aviation Gin
1 ½ oz Celery Tonic*
½ oz lime juice
lime

Combine ingredients with a whopping scoop of ice in a blender. Blend that shit until smooth. Garnish with a lime wheel and try not to set the kitchen on fire.

*Celery Tonic

3 c sugar
2 c water
6 tbsp citric acid
3 tbsp quassia bark chips
2 orange peels
4 stalks of lemon grass (smashed)
3 limes (zested and juiced)
8 stalks celery (juiced)

Add the sugar and water in a saucepan and start heating that shit up. Dump all the other stuff in and simmer over medium heat until you feel good about it. Remove and fine strain with a cheese cloth.

Oh, and it's pronounced KASS-YA, dummy.

Tools: blender, jigger, paring knife, wide peeler, juicer, wooden spoon or beer bottle (for smashing)

CHAPTER TWO:
BRINGIN' 'TINI BACK

Remember the days of cocktail menus boasting everything in an "up" glass and names ending in "'tini"? Yeah, we do too. It's where Dustin got his start behind the bar. Plastic bottles of sour mix, Hershey's sauce, blue stuff, green stuff... oh my! We aren't the kind to run from our pasts; we're here to embrace it and bring that shit back! Anyone that tells you a modern-day well-made *Cosmo* or *Appletini* with fresh ingredients is silly needs a swift kick in the pants. If there's one thing us ding dongs know, it's that everything deserves a second chance, especially that disastrous cocktail trend we remember as the "'Tini Days."

KEEP IT FRESH! USE FRESH CITRUS, NOT BOTTLED.

FRENCH MARTINI

French Martini

1 ½ oz Ketel One Vodka
½ oz Berry-Berry Ding Dong Liqueur*
1 oz pineapple juice
½ oz lemon juice

Combine all your ingredients in the shaker tin. Add ice and shake that shit up! Strain with your hawthorne into your 'tini glass and talk amongst yourselves. Here's a topic: "I made that liqueur there. This bartending thing is so easy..." Discuss. Don't even bother garnishing it.

*Berry-Berry Ding Dong Liqueur

1 bottle of vodka
2 c white sugar
peels from 2 lemons
1 tsp citric acid
2 c berries of your choice (chopped)

Let these ingredients sit in a dark, scary, terrifying room (or just on your kitchen counter) for three to five days in a sealable jar. Agitate daily by shaking it like it owes you money. Fine strain and serve it up! Keep refrigerated if you don't drink it all at once.

Tools: shaker tin, hawthorne strainer, jigger, wide peeler, paring knife

APPLETINI

Appletini

2 oz Calvados Apple Brandy
1 oz lemon juice
1 oz simple syrup
cherry

Even the biggest dingaling can't mess this one up! Shake all those ingredients up and strain into (you guessed it) your 'tini glass. Garnish with a cherry or a lemon twist. Don't let me catch you using those nasty ass red dye #40 cherries, neither. Michigan cherries or bust.

Tools: shaker tin, hawthorne strainer, jigger, channel knife

Cosmopolitan

1½ oz Absolut Vodka
¾ oz Combier Orange Curaçao
½ oz lime juice
1½ oz tart cranberry juice
orange

Yes, we mean that drink from that show about four single working ladies from a little unknown island in New York and probably your auntie's go-to cocktail. Take your shaker and put all that shit in there with ice. Shake it up and strain into a chilled 'tini glass. You can chill the glass by putting it in the fridge, or if you're as lazy as we are, by filling it with ice water before you shake up your ingredients. Finish with an orange twist garnish or a swath.

Tools: shaker tin, hawthorne strainer, jigger, channel knife or wide peeler

GIBSON

Gibson

2 oz Grey Goose Vodka
1 oz Vya Dry Vermouth
1 Pickled Onion*

Stir in a mixing glass and strain with your julep strainer. Garnish with the hippest pickled onion.

*Pickled Onion

Don't panic, dingaling, but we're going to pickle the shit outta some onions. Grab a medium saucepan and combine:

2 c white wine vinegar
2 c water
¼ c salt
1 tsp sugar
1 cinnamon stick
4 juniper berries
2 allspice pods
1 tbsp cayenne pepper
2 bay leaves
2 fresh rosemary skewers
1 pinch of marjoram
1 big ol' handful of fresh dill

Bring to a slow simmer to heat the liquid, then strain into a sealable mason jar with one pound of pearl onions. Let cool to room temperature, cover tightly and refrigerate.

Tools: mixing glass, bar spoon, julep strainer, jigger

SUMMER VESPER

Summer Vesper

1 oz Grey Goose Vodka
1 oz Bombay Sapphire Gin
1 oz Lillet Rosé Aperitif Wine
3 dashes rhubarb bitters
lemon

Don't listen to James Bond. Stir that shit for sure. Add a lemon swath or a twist or James Bond VHS tape as a garnish. I don't give a shit.

Tools: mixing glass, bar spoon, julep strainer, jigger, wide peeler or channel knife

GIN MARTINI

Classic Gin Martini

2 oz Bombay Sapphire Gin
1 oz dry vermouth (Dolin Blanc is smooth as hell)
2 dashes Bittercube Orange Bitters
orange

Next dingaling to debate us on the history of the martini is gonna
find themselves in a nasty tickle fight with us. Put your booze and
bitters in a mixing glass and add ice, stir with your bar spoon
(this is probably going to take you forever since stirring is hard, so
practice!), strain, and garnish with orange oils from a fat orange
swath.

Tools: mixing glass, bar spoon, julep strainer, jigger, wide peeler

CHOGOLATINI

Chocolatini

1 ½ oz Brugal Extra Dry Rum
½ oz crème de cacao liqueur
1 ½ oz Chocolate Mousse*
4 drops vanilla extract

Dear ding dong, please take all these calorie-free ingredients and shake them up! Strain into your 'tini glass with zero guilt and zero shame. Garnish with a side of diet cola. See what I did there?

*Chocolate Mousse

Ding dongs plus fire equals we're not liable... But hell, in a medium saucepan add:

1 ½ c unsweetened cocoa powder
1 ½ c white sugar
1 c heavy whipping cream
peels from 2 oranges
1 tsp Versa Whip

Cook on low heat until the first four ingredients are integrated, let cool and add to a blender with the Versa Whip. Blend until frothy.

Tools: shaker tin, hawthorne strainer, jigger, blender

DIRTY MARTINI

Dirty Martini

2 oz vodka or gin... who really gives a shit?
½ oz dry vermouth
1½ oz filthy olive brine (the foggy water in the jar of olives you have in the back of your fridge)
olive

Take your ingredients and shake them until you get bored! Strain into your 'tini glass and garnish with whatever gross pickled shit you have in your fridge. No, but really, garnish with olives.

Tools: shaker tin, hawthorne strainer, jigger

EL CAPITAN

El Capitan

2 oz Control Pisco
1 oz Cinzano Vermouth
3 dashes Amargo Bitters
1 finely minced pickled pearl onion*
orange

OMG! Don't be so dramatic! Yes, you're gonna mince a pearl onion with a paring knife, put it in a mixing glass with the rest of the ingredients, then add ice and stir. Fine strain into a footed rocks glass. Squeeze some orange oils on top from a fat swath.

Tools: mixing glass, bar spoon, julep strainer, paring knife, fine strainer

*See Gibson, page 41

GIMLET

Gimlet ('tini)

2 oz Aviation Gin or Rehorst Vodka
¾ oz lime juice
¾ oz simple syrup
lime

If you can't figure what to do with these ingredients, ding dong, this book is probably in the right hands. That's right, shake that shit up and strain into a 'tini glass. Cut yourself off a nice piece of lime (we like a sexy wheel) and garnish.

Tools: shaker tin, jigger, hawthorne strainer, paring knife

LEMON DROP

Lemon Drop

1½ oz Absolut Citron Vodka
½ oz limoncello
½ oz simple syrup
¾ oz lemon juice
lemon

Oh, great. They got us making lemon drops now?! Actually, this dumb dumb-'tini is marvelous when made right, so don't mess it up! Take all that shit and shake it up! Strain it into your 'tini glass with a big ol' lemon twist garnish or a swath. Drink it in private. (Secret's safe with us.)

Tools: shaker tin, hawthorne strainer, jigger, channel knife or wide peeler

CHAPTER THREE:
AGED 'N' SEXY

You're an adult now, or at least you're striving to be. Either way, grow up! This volume is all about spoiling yourself because we all know how hard it is to be an adult. So don't be a cheap ass. Next time you're at the liquor store, splurge a little. Treat yourself to that añejo tequila or that Pappy Van Winkle you've always wanted. If you see no need for this, move along to Chapter Four because I'm done with you.

DISCLAIMER: Though we highly recommend using our suggested spirits in the recipes, feel free to sub in something more wallet friendly. We'll judge from afar.

BLOOD & SAND

Blood & Sand

¾ oz Glenfiddich 15 Year Scotch
¾ oz sweet vermouth (Try with Punt e Mes. It's the shit.)
¾ oz Cherry Heering Liqueur
¾ oz orange juice
orange

Add this business together in your shaker. Shake the shit out of it and double strain with your hawthorne strainer into a chilled footed rocks glass. Garnish it with baby seal blood or an orange swath… whatever's handy.

Tools: shaker tin, hawthorne strainer, fine strainer, jigger, wide peeler

SCOFFLAW

Scofflaw

1½ oz Rittenhouse Rye Whiskey
1 oz Carpano Dry Vermouth
¾ oz lemon juice
¾ oz House Grenadine*
lemon

You should feel like a real badass making this drink! Sort of "above the law" if you're doing it right. So without giving a shit throw all those ingredients into your shaker with ice! Shake that shit and double strain into a chilled champagne saucer. Using your channel knife, give it a big ol' lemon twist and make sure that cocktail knows you're the boss.

*House Grenadine

2 c pomegranate juice
1 c sugar
peel from 1 orange
1 cinnamon stick

It's super easy to make your own grenadine. In a medium saucepan on low heat lazily stir all those ingredients. Cook until sugar is dissolved, let cool to room temperature, then strain. Store in a squeeze bottle for easy use.

Tools: shaker tin, hawthorne strainer, fine strainer, jigger, wide peeler

FRENCH 75

French 75

2 oz Hennessy VSOP Cognac
½ oz House Sugar*
½ oz lemon juice
Moët & Chandon
orange

You probably just blew your paycheck on these ingredients, but you're a grown dingaling, so let's move past it. In your Boston shaker, add the first three ingredients with ice. Shake that shit real slow and sexy, double strain with your fine strainer into a chilled champagne flute, and top with the bottle of Moët. (Pop the cork with a sword if you really wanna impress somebody.) Take that channel knife and make a large lemon twist to throw in that shit. How baller do you feel right now?

Tools: hawthorne strainer, shaker tin, fine strainer, channel knife

*See Sazerac, page 23

ROB ROY

Rob Roy

2 oz Glenmorangie La Santa 10 Year Scotch
1 oz sweet vermouth (Try Carpano Antica. It's classy as hell.)
3 dashes Angostura Bitters
lemon

Add all these fancy pants ingredients into a mixing glass. Using your bar spoon, stir like you've never stirred before. Better yet, just stir with your finger, dumb dumb! Strain into a chilled footed rocks glass and garnish with expressed lemon oils, or a cherry, or a sword… it's still classy as hell.

Tools: mixing glass, bar spoon, julep strainer, jigger, wide peeler

OLD FASHIONED

Old Fashioned

2 oz Four Roses Single Barrel Bourbon
2 dashes Bittercube Orange Bitters
2 dashes Angostura Bitters
¼ oz House Sugar*

First off: kick on some Marvin Gaye.

We'll wait.

Okay, now serenade the ingredients while you pour them into your mixing glass. Add ice and stir, stir, stir, ding dong! Strain that sexy elixir into a double old fashioned glass full of fatty cubes, express orange and lemon oils from some swaths and drop those peels into that shit.

Tools: mixing glass, bar spoon, julep strainer, jigger, wide peeler

See Sazerac, page 23

Last Word

1 oz Bombay Sapphire Gin
¾ oz Green Chartreuse
½ oz Luxardo Maraschino Liqueur
¾ oz lime juice
cherry

If Buddha were to make you a drink, this would probably be the
one. That green stuff that just set you back a pretty penny is
made by monks, so it's basically sanctioned by the church. Add
all these adult liquids to your shaker with ice, shake the livin' shit
out of it, and double strain with your fine strainer into a chilled
champagne saucer. Don't even think about garnishing this shit!
Well. That's not true. You can throw a cherry in it if you must. But
it's also perfect without it.

Tools: shaker tin, hawthorne strainer, fine strainer, jigger, paring
knife

HEMINGWAY DAIQUIRI

Hemingway Daiquiri

1½ oz Bacardi 8 Year Aged Rum
½ oz Luxardo Maraschino Liqueur
¾ oz lime juice
¾ oz grapefruit juice
lime

Things we have in common with Hemingway:

1) Diabetes
2) We're super famous authors
3) We're Illinois natives
4) We love the hooch!

So out of respect to this dude, shake all this shit up in your Boston shaker with ice. Fine strain into a champagne saucer and garnish with a lime wheel. "You like apples? How you like dem apples?" — (totally not) Ernest Hemingway

Tools: shaker tin, hawthorne strainer, fine strainer, jigger, paring knife

Bon V's Margarita

1½ oz Tequila Ocho Reposado
1 oz Combier Orange Curaçao
¾ oz lime juice
1 barspoon agave nectar
lime
coarse salt (optional)

Take all this shit and shake it up together with some ice, dingaling! If you want some salt on that shit, you gotta work for it. Take a lime wedge and rub it around the top of your glass (use a double old fashioned or triple the recipe and put that sweet elixir in a mason jar). Liberally salt a plate, turn the glass upside down, and dip the glass to salt the rim. Strain with a hawthorne strainer and garnish with a lime wheel.

Tools: shaker tin, hawthorne strainer, jigger, paring knife, saucer

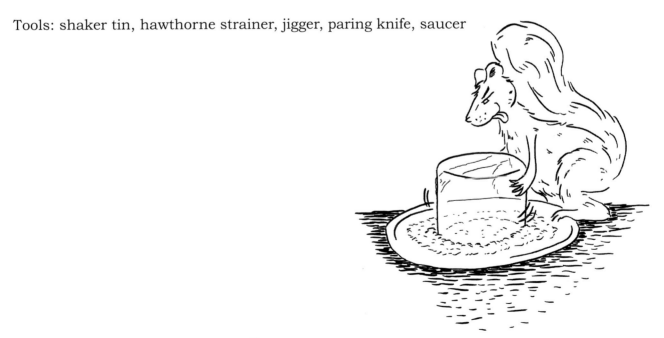

SIDECAR

Sidecar

1½ oz Hennessy VSOP Cognac
¾ oz Cointreau
¾ oz lemon juice
1 big ol' bar spoon confectioner's sugar
orange

In your Boston shaker add all this shit with ice and shake it up. Put the sugar on a plate, rub an orange slice around half the rim of a 'tini glass, and dip that shit in the sugar. Fine strain into your diabete-dusted 'tini glass, use your wide peeler to peel off a wide orange swath, express those oils, and drop that shit in.

Tools: shaker tin, hawthorne strainer, fine strainer, jigger, saucer, wide peeler

VIEUX CARRÉ

Vieux Carré

¾ oz Bulleit Rye Whiskey
¾ oz Carpano Antica Sweet Vermouth
¾ oz Hennessy VSOP Cognac
¼ oz Bénédictine
2 dashes Peychaud's bitters
2 dashes Angostura bitters

Stop trying to pronounce this cocktail, you're embarrassing yourself. French vowels are hard, especially when you've been mixing cocktails. Let's just move forward, shall we? In your mixing glass, add all ingredients, then some ice, and stir with your bar spoon to chill this son of a bitch down. Strain over an iced rocks glass. Using your wide peeler (don't lose a finger, please!), remove a large peel of lemon, and express them oils over the cocktail. Enjoy.

Tools: mixing glass, bar spoon, julep strainer, wide peeler, jigger

CHAPTER FOUR:
BEACH DON'T KILL MY VIBE

Whether or not it's summer, we are firm believers in transporting ourselves to places that require cocktails. In this case, grab your arm floaties and water socks—it's time to hit the beach! Let's keep in mind these aren't those bastardized recipes you're used to drankin' during the double bubble buy-one-get-diabetes happy hour from your local steakhouse chain, so you're gonna have to trust me here. We gon' be alright...

(PSA: We here at *Cocktails for Ding Dongs* highly recommend *not* getting shit faced and trying to conquer Lake Michigan. In other words, don't get hammered and go for a swim, dingaling. And please don't get wasted and pilot a boat. Please.)

MAI TAI

Mai Tai

1 oz Brugal Extra Dry Rum
1 oz Rhum Agricole
¾ oz Small Hands Orgeat Syrup
¾ oz lime juice
2 dashes Angostura Bitters
pineapple
mint

Add all these things that you probably can't pronounce to your shaker tin and add ice. Shake and strain with your hawthorne into an obnoxious fancy glass full of ice. Cut up a pineapple and garnish with a large mint bushel. Or double the recipe and throw the damn drink into a hollowed-out pineapple. The beauty of tiki cocktails is in their flexibility. And large containers.

Tools: shaker tin, hawthorne strainer, jigger, paring knife

FOG GUTTER

Fog Cutter

1½ oz Bacardi Superior Rum
½ oz gin
½ oz Copper & Kings Brandy
½ oz Amontillado Sherry
1½ oz orange juice
1 oz lemon juice
½ oz Small Hands Orgeat Syrup
orange

Holy shit! That's a lot of stuff to conjure up, isn't it? Well, don't be scared, dingaling: we're putting it all in our Boston shaker with ice and shaking the shit out of it. Let's do ye ol' "slop and dump," which means: just pour it right from your shaker into a fancy tiki glass. You don't even need to strain! Surprise yourself with the garnish on this one; we really don't give a shit how your garnish your drink. It's all good. But if you like being told what to do, use an orange slice.

Tools: shaker tin, jigger, paring knife

PIÑA COLADA

Piña Colada

1½ oz Brugal Extra Dry Rum
½ oz Ed Hamilton Gold Cask Rum
1 oz cream
1½ oz Pineapple Gomme*
pineapple
cherry

If you don't own a blender, grab the thingy you make your smoothies in, maybe something you bought from some late night infomercial. Add all ingredients, a bunch of ice, and rip that shit up! Strain into that big ol' obnoxious glass. Add a pineapple wedge and cherry. Oh, and a fancy umbrella. And shit, if you want some aromatics, grate some nutmeg on top with a microplane. Do it, do it right now, ding dong!

*Pineapple Gomme

1 qt pineapple juice
2 c sugar
1 tsp gum arabic powder

Grab some goggles and a snorkel just in case, put these ingredients in a saucepan, cook at real low heat, whisking aggressively with (you guessed it) a whisk, the whole damn time. Remove from heat and let cool to room temperature. If I have to explain why it should be room temperature, this book is totally for you.

Tools: jigger, blender, patio furniture, microplane, paring knife.

Mojito

1 oz Brugal Extra Dry Rum
1 oz Brugal Añejo Rum
¾ oz House Sugar*
¾ oz lime juice
6-8 mint leaves
3 oz H_2O with CO_2

We are gonna disrupt some cell walls in that mint. Place it in the palm of your hand and slap that shit! Put it in a collins glass. With a muddler, move those mint leaves up and down that glass real slow and creepy like. You can also use the back of the bar spoon if you're a savage and don't own a muddler. Now add the rest of your ingredients and top with ice and a big ol' mint bushel garnish.
Give it a lazy stir to cool it off. Way to go, ding dong. You did it!

Tools: jigger, muddler, bar spoon

*See Sazerac, page 23

PAINKILLER

Painkiller

2 oz Pusser's Rum (please don't sue us!)
1 oz pineapple juice
1 oz orange juice
½ oz cream of coconut
grated nutmeg

Put all these liquids into your Boston shaker with ice and shake that shit up! Strain over a tall iced tiki glass. Using a microplane, grate some fresh nutmeg over the finished cocktail. No, really, that's it. Now you can go back to getting shit faced.

Tools: shaker tin, jigger, hawthorne strainer, microplane

Light 'n' Cloudy

2 oz dark rum
1 lime
3 oz ginger beer
2 hearty dashes Angostura bitters

This looks simple enough, right? Oh, but wait, we're going to build this bad boy backwards. Get yourself a collins glass and place that shit right in front of you. Cut a lime in half. Using your hand or a hand press, squeeze the juice of half a lime into the collins glass. Save the other half because it'll be your garnish, dingaling! Add ginger beer and ice all the way to the top of the glass, place the half shell into the cocktail, then add the rum on top. If it's a good dark rum, and you pour it slowly, it'll float on top and look classy as hell.

Tools: jigger, paring knife, hand press

ZOMBIE ISLAND!

Zombie Island!

1½ oz Bacardi Superior Rum
½ oz Ed Hamilton Black Cask Rum
1 manicured apricot (or sub 1 oz apricot liqueur)
1 ½ oz Pineapple Gomme*
1 oz lime juice
mint
lime

First things first: I hope it's stone fruit season, but if not, just sub in an apricot liqueur in its place. De-seed that piece of fruit and cut it into quarters, grab your muddler, and smash it in the shaker tin. Add your remaining ingredients with ice and shake it up! Using your fine strainer, pour over an iced obnoxious tiki glass, then garnish with a mint bushel and lime wheel, dingaling!

Tools: jigger, muddler, shaker tin, paring knife, hawthorne strainer, fine strainer

*See Piña Colada, page 85

CORN 'N' OIL

Corn 'n' Oil

1 oz Ed Hamilton Black Cask Rum
1 oz Bitter Truth Golden Falernum
juice from 1 lime

Remove the peel from a lime with a wide peeler. Holding the lime with your finger and thumb on each end, start at the top of the fruit, rotate it while peeling all the way down to remove the whole peel. (We know, we know. It's hard, but it's super impressive at parties, so practice.) Hold on to this green donkey tail; it's your garnish! Now cut that lime in half and juice that shit into your Boston shaker with your hand press. Add your rum, falernum, and ice, and shake that hooch up! Strain over an iced old fashioned glass, then wrap the lime peel around the inside of the glass.

Tools: jigger, paring knife, wide peeler, shaker tin, hawthorne strainer

BEACHCOMBER

The Beachcomber

1½ oz rum
½ oz Combier Orange Curaçao
¼ oz Luxardo Maraschino Liqueur
¾ oz lime juice
1 hearty bar spoon white sugar

Put all this shit into your Boston shaker with ice and shake up
this legendary cocktail. Strain into an old fashioned glass full
of ice, and with your wide peeler, remove a large orange swath.
Express the oils over the cocktail, then drop the swath in. Nailed
it!

Tools: jigger, shaker tin, bar spoon, hawthorne strainer

GLOSSARY

TOOLS

Channel Knife

Bar Spoon

Microplane

Wide Peeler

Paring Knife

Hawthorne Strainer

Julep Strainer

Mixing Glass

Muddler

Boston Shaker

Fine Strainer

Jigger

Hand Press

GLASSES

 Collins

 Champagne Flute

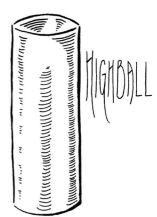 Highball

 Martini

 Footed Rocks

 Shot

 Champagne Saucer

 Cordial

 Hurricane

 Double Old Fashioned

 Rocks

 Snifter

GADGETS

SMOKING
GUN

ISI CARBONATOR

JUICER

SPIRITS

Absinthe

Letherbee

A distilled, highly alcoholic, anise-flavored spirit flavored with botanicals, notably wormwood, anise, and fennel. Absinthe was banned in the US in 1915 because it was thought to be a hallucinogen but has undergone a revival due to modernized beverage laws enacted in the 1990's.

Bitters

Amargo, Angostura, Bittercube Orange, Bittercube Vanilla-Cherry Bark, Fee Brothers Rhubarb, Peychaud's, Scrappy's Chocolate

Bitters are traditionally an alcoholic preparation flavored with herbs, roots, barks and other botanical ingredients. They have a highly concentrated flavor profile and are often considered the "salt and pepper" of the cocktail world.

Blended Whiskey

Cutty Sark Prohibition Blended Scotch

A blended whiskey is the product of blending different types of whiskeys and sometimes also neutral grain spirits, coloring, and flavorings. A blended scotch will generally have a mellower flavor than a single malt scotch.

Bourbon

Four Roses Single Barrel, Rebel Yell

A category of whiskey which must be made in the USA and consist of at least 51% corn mash, aged in new charred oak barrels for at least 2 years. U.S.A! U.S.A! U.S.A!

Brandy

Copper & Kings

A distilled wine, always made from grapes, and often matured in wooden casks.

Cognac

Hennessy VSOP

A high quality brandy made in the Cognac region of western France. Must be aged at least 2 years in Limousin oak casks.

Eau De Vie

Calvados, Control Pisco

A category of brandy, a distilled spirit that is made from fruits other than grapes like apples, pears or cherries. Means "water of life" in French.

Gin

Aviation, Bombay Sapphire

A clear alcoholic spirit distilled from grain or malt and flavored with juniper berries. Specific gins are either defined as "floral" (on the sweeter side) or "dry." There are many different styles of gin and we highly recommend geeking out and learning all about them if you're interested.

Liqueur

Bénédictine, Bitter Truth Golden Falernum, Cherry Heering, Combier Fruits de Rouge, Combier Orange Curaçao, Cointreau, crème de noyaux, crème de cacao, Green Chartreuse, Luxardo Maraschino, Zucca Amaro

A liqueur is an alcoholic beverage made from a distilled spirit that has been flavored with fruit, cream, herbs, spices, flowers or nuts and bottled with added sugar or other sweetener. They can range from the very sweet (such as Cherry Heering) to very bitter (any liqueur labeled *amaro*, which means "bitter" in Italian).

Rum

Bacardi 8, Bacardi Superior, Brugal Añejo, Brugal Extra Dry, Ed Hamilton Black Cask, Ed Hamilton Gold Cask, Pusser's, Rhum Agricole

An alcoholic spirit distilled from sugar-cane residues or molasses. Pirates are super into it. Can range from clear and dry to dark as motor oil and quite sweet.

Rye

Bulleit, Rebel Yell, Rittenhouse

A category of whiskey in which the mash by law must consist of 51% rye, aged in new charred oak barrels for at least 2 years. 'Murica!

Scotch

Glenfiddich 15, Glenmorangie La Santa 12, Laphroaig 10

In a nutshell, it is a category of whiskey widely produced in Scotland from a mash of malted barley aged at least 3 years in barrels. Some commercial production will use wheat or rye for their mash. Often has a smokey/peaty taste and smell due to the barley grown in Scotland. Can be single malt or blended.

Tequila

Suerte Reposado Tequila, Tequila Ocho Reposado

A Mexican spirit made from 100% blue agave and commonly seen in villages surrounding the city of Tequila in the state of Jalisco. Ranges from clear (silver or *plata* or *blanco*) to *reposado* (rested/aged for a brief period), to *añejo* (aged for a longer period).

Vermouth/Fortified Wine

Amontillado Sherry, Carpano Antica, Carpano Dry, Cinzano, Dolin Blanc, Lillet Rosé, Punt e Mes, Vya Dry, White Port

A red or white wine flavored with aromatic herbs, fruits and/or spices, and fortified with distilled spirits (often brandy), made primarily in France and Italy. Commonly used as a mixer in cocktails, but may also be consumed alone as an *aperitif* before a meal.

Vodka

Absolut, Absolut Citron, Grey Goose, Ketel One, Rehorst

A clear alcoholic spirit that can be distilled from basically anything, although it's usually made from cereal grains or potatoes. Can be flavored with pretty much anything.

THE AUTHORS

Raised in a small farm town in northern Wisconsin, Dustin Drankiewicz began his hospitality career at age fourteen at the only sit-down restaurant in town, where he was fired for dying his hair green. He served stints bartending in Milwaukee and Las Vegas before settling down in Chicago to serve classically-inspired cocktails at all manner of seedy establishments.

Alexandra Ensign studied cinema and media studies at the University of Chicago before becoming a bartender, loyal civil servant, and cartoonist, with a passion for mixing cocktails and putting the inking in drinking. She spends her free time working very, very slowly on her graphic novel, trolling her cats, and making comics, zines, and illustrations. You can check out some of her work at www.alexandraensign.com.